8 0   Y E A R S   O F   F U N

When the comics team started work on The Beano back in 1937, they could have had no idea they were creating a British pop culture icon. Now in its 80th year, The Beano is officially recognised as the world's longest-running weekly comic, and has been delighting children for generations!

This collection of Beano history selects eight single issues – to capture snapshots of different eras of the comic, using each one to discuss The Beano's cultural impact more widely, whether through the prism of the Second World War, free gifts, or its most famous son – Dennis the Menace.

With nearly 4,000 issues and counting to choose from, selecting just eight was an unenviable task. The eight issues herein all capture that indefinable Beano magic and help us to understand the wider socio-political landscape and cultural trends of the times.

I hope you enjoy the journey!

John Anderson, Editor
April, 2018

Some pages may contain references which are of their time,
but would not be considered suitable today.

BIG EGGO IS HATCHED

Beano No. 1 // July 30th, 1938

1938 was a funny old year… the top pop song was 'The Biggest Aspidistra in the World' and footballing giants Grimsby Town finished tenth in the First Division, the Premier League of the time. But in July it got a lot funnier when The Beano hit the streets!

Published on 30th July, 1938, and costing just two old pence, it was 28 pages of funny comic strips mixed with the occasional adventure prose story. The undoubted star was Big Eggo, a zany ostrich forever looking for his egg! Through early correspondence between the head of D.C. Thomson's children's department, R.D. Low, and artist Reg Carter, we can trace Eggo's journey from the glimmering of an idea to the front page of the first-ever Beano!

Originally conceived of as the second of five planned humour comics (The Dandy being the first), it was quite the undertaking to find illustrators to fill the pages of five comics every week! So Low placed an ad in the periodical of choice for artists the world over at that time — The Daily Telegraph.

On 15th January, 1938, artist Reg Carter responded…

> In reply to your Advertisement in yesterday's Telegraph, I am sending a few ideas for Comic Strips , all I have by me at moment.

REG CARTER

Reg Carter was a very experienced artist, a prolific comic postcard illustrator and had humorous strips with a host of other publications including the Mickey Mouse comic, which launched in 1930. R.D. Low thought Carter's robust drawings were perfect for a comic cover. The pair worked closely together experimenting with several new animal characters. Low sent lengthy letters to Sussex-based Carter, explaining what he was looking for and Carter for his part returned many, many experimental sketches. Eventually the choice came down to an ostrich or a gorilla. The bird got the nod and Big Eggo, the ostrich who was constantly looking for his egg, graced the first Beano cover. Carter would continue drawing for The Beano for the next decade.

The first ever Beano comic — featuring Big Eggo on the cover!

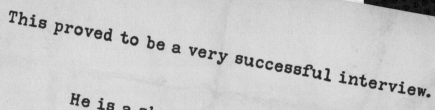

This proved to be a very successful interview.

Low was immediately impressed after interviewing Carter in person at D.C. Thomson's Fleet Street office. Low was an exhaustive note taker and recorded the meeting in this report from early 1938…

He is a sharp, capable chap, 45 or so. Used to work with Ally Sloper and was on Monster Comic with Mansfield whom you may remember.

Has a fine line of work on Mickey Mouse and A.P and also does really nice colour work for calendars for Valentine. His work is clean and he is very willing to do a lot for us.

I fixed on several ostrich and some ape sets and also got two glimmerings of ideas…

He couldn't decide which would make the better character — an ape or an ostrich. He eventually settled upon the ostrich, despite the counsel of his young children who thought this was a crazy idea! He shared this idea with Carter in a letter on 12th February, 1938.

My idea for the other series would be round a comical ostrich. The ostrich lends itself readily to all sorts of fun, and I have also jotted down a few ideas that would work up round this character. I would, of course, like to se⎯⎯ ⎯⎯ sketch of the ostrich for the purpose of ge⎯⎯ ⎯⎯ ⎯ould not ask for a caricature ⎯⎯ of an ostrich wi⎯ about him.

OSWALD THE OSTRICH

The idea is to get a very 'human' ostri⎯ up to all the characteristics of an ostrich hide its head in the sand, kick like a mule, A good touch might be got out of Oswald alway⎯ for an egg he has lost.

Soon, the ostrich had a name… Oswald!

And so The Beano's first cover star was born! However, Carter's first illustration was not met with enthusiasm by Low, as you can read in this letter from 17th February, 1938. ———

Carter's reply was recorded just two days later on 19th February, which is amazing considering there was no email! All of the scripts and artwork were sent via snail mail between the two. In this context, the speed at which the letters went back and forth was fantastic — and probably wore out those poor snails!

Thanks for your rough of "Oswald The Ostrich".

I am afraid I may have misled you in my previous letter, because now that I see your suggestion I can only say I would far rather see a more caricatured type of bird. You could afford to be almost ludicrous, with big feet and big goggled eyes and plenty of exaggerated expression on the face.

I am afraid that I am at fault here, but I am sure you will see what I am driving at when I suggest that you let yourself go with Oswald and caricature the ostrich to your heart's content.

Many thanks for yours of 17th inst., I am sorry I misunderstood your instructions as to the ostrich, and now send you 2 new sketches. I can improve on these as I go along, as as far as I can remember I have only done one drawing of this quaint bird before and that years ago. the sketch sent first, I took from a book of photographs of the London Zoo, the head is ridiculously small in reality, and I think to get any expression at all, must be caricatured. If new drawings not quite as you would like, I will have another shot.

I find it somewhat difficult working so small. but shall get used to it, the same in Archie set, one of which I send, this I am not pleased with, there again I felt rather hemmed in, and trust next set will shew much improvement.

Low gave Carter the instruction to 'let yourself go', and Carter was soon submitting more roughs. Unfortunately for us, Low always sent these sketches to Carter by return, so while we can see the feedback, those early sketches have been long since lost to history. Low met with Carter at the Fleet Street office once more, which seems to have aided the development, as Carter's final letter on 12th March, 1938, reveals.

Reference our conversation at your London Office last week. I am sending finished sketches to the rough ideas passed, also to the first rough sent you of Oswald, as think I am beginning to get hold of him, if you think the eyes need more "goggling" I can do this in future drawings.

d play
anything,
ast.
king

He needn't have worried, as his new illustrations were to Low's satisfaction and further 'goggling' was not required! Big Eggo was born!

When **R.D. Low** was puzzling over the pieces that he hoped would gel together and form The Beano, he was only certain of one thing — what style of cover he wanted. It would be an animal character, predominantly black and white and on a very highly coloured background. This was the formula he had used for the Korky the Cat strip on the cover of The Dandy and it had proved popular and very eye-catching.

Big Eggo was The Beano's first cover star, and would be forever hunting his lost egg for the first ten years of the comic, eventually being replaced by another black and white animal, Biffo the Bear, in 1948!

With the cover star now in place, the countdown to publication began! It was marketed across a number of D.C. Thomson titles, which included eight-page mini comics heralding the new arrival. Boys' adventure papers, The Wizard and Adventure did so, as you would expect, but also The People's Friend — hardly the natural home for young boys seeking the thrill of slapstick, mischief and adventure!

Even big brother, The Dandy got in on the act, although with considerably less fanfare. The Dandy office was just a few short steps down the corridor from The Beano office, and unfortunately what The Dandy team really thought goes unrecorded...

What else was in No. 1?

No. 1 featured a mix of comic strips and adventure prose stories. Some of the comic strips wore their influences on their sleeves, such as 'Here Comes Ping the Elastic Man' and 'Brave Captain Kipper', which were close in style to the American newspaper 'funnies' of the time.

It is in the funnies that we see The Beano's British sense of humour shine through, and where it most closely resembles the comic today. 'Wee Peem', 'Little Dead-Eye Dick' and 'Helpful Henry' are funny slapstick strips about mischievous kids who would come to popularise the comic after the war. The most famous of these was 'Lord Snooty and His Pals', which saw the young Marmaduke, Earl of Bunkerton, escape from Bunkerton Castle to play with his true pals, the kids from Ash-Can Alley. Beano readers would have identified with the playful working-class kids and understood why Snooty liked them.

A large proportion of the pages were given over to the prose stories, however, with 'Morgyn the Mighty', 'The Adventures of Tom Thumb', 'The Wishing Tree', 'The Shipwrecked Kidds', 'My Dog Sandy', 'The Ape's Secret' and 'Wild Boy of the Woods' providing plenty of adventure alongside the paragraphs of tiny type! They are all born from the stable of adventure fiction pioneered by the likes of Edgar Rice Burroughs, but would gradually be replaced by more humour strips.

D.C. Thomson's new comics, including The Beano, would revolutionise the children's papers market. Their rival Amalgamated Press, who published Comic Cuts and Illustrated Chips, and who would later become Fleetway Publications, published their comics in a tabloid format.

D.C. Thomson had other plans. Their comics were a more compact size and were longer at 28 pages. This new format, inspired by American-style comics, felt like a higher value publication but for the same price (two pence) as the Amalgamated Press comics.

D.C. Thomson's new publishing mix didn't stop at paper stock. The design was also innovative. Looking to America, the comic teams created covers with colourful artwork and ballooned stories instead of the British tradition of illustrations with blocks of text underneath. D.C. Thomson's strategy worked and the launch of The Beano and its brother, The Dandy, marked the beginning of the decline of boys' adventure papers and the dominance of comics in the UK.

How do we judge the success of Low and Carter's work in creating Eggo… and the rest of the characters for that first Beano? The first issue sold 443,000 copies, and as we fast approach the 4,000th issue in 2019, it seems like an odd question to ask. Fortunately, The Beano office was very quickly inundated with sackfuls of fan mail, some of which ended up in the archives. These are contemporary pieces of fan mail, never seen before, and show how the readers immediately identified with the comic's mischievous characters. As buying a stamp in 1938 to send a letter to the office in Dundee would probably have cost most of an average child's pocket money in 1938 (much like now!), this was a genuine act of devotion at the time!

The characters recorded in these 80 year-old letters included Wee Peem, Lord Snooty, Big Fat Joe and, of course, Big Eggo. In fact, nearly every character is covered in some way.

The comics I like best are young strong arm, and In the land of the silver dwarfs. I like the rest too, and Wee Pem sure is a proper scream

Yours Truly
Edward McGregor

■ One of the most interesting early letters comes from Edward McGregor from Ontario, Canada!

■ His favourite character was Wee Peem. Needless to say, the exploding cigar would not make it past today's editorial team.

WEE PEEM

HE'S A PROPER SCREAM

■ Joyce Moore from Burnley wrote to tell us she thought Lord Snooty was very funny. He appeared in every issue until 1991! This is part of that first strip from No. 1.

I like best in The Beano Big Fat Joe, and Big Egg.

THE GOLDEN AGE OF COMICS

The 1930s heralded a new era of comics and introduced characters to the world that we still know and love.

January, 1930 MICKEY MOUSE
Launching in January 1930, the Mickey Mouse daily comic strip was originally scripted by Walt Disney and drawn by Ub Iwerks.

January, 1934 FLASH GORDON
Created by King Features Syndicate in order to compete with the already established Buck Rogers adventure strip, Flash Gordon first appeared alongside Jungle Jim.

December, 1937 THE DANDY
Issue one of The Dandy launched with a Korky The Cat strip on the cover. Less than a year after its debut, the first Dandy Annual was released.

June, 1938 SUPERMAN
Created by writer Jerry Siegel and artist Joe Shuster in 1933, Superman was first published by Detective Comics (D.C.) in 1938 in their newly-launched Action Comics.

July, 1938 THE BEANO
The longest-running weekly comic in the world launched in summer 1938, joining its brother title The Dandy which launched only seven months earlier.

1939 ARCHIE COMICS, FAWCETT, FOX FEATURE SYNDICATE, DETECTIVE COMICS (LATER D.C.) AND TIMELY PUBLICATIONS (LATER MARVEL)
With the successful launch of Superman, the American market began to grow — and quickly. Before the decade was out readers were introduced to legendary titles such as Batman and Marvel Mystery Comics.

He Hasn't Been Weighed Since the Age of Three —The Weighing-Machine Always Broke, You See.

BIG FAT JOE

In case Brian is still a fan, here's Big Fat Joe, getting his own back on the bullies!

Robert D. Low

'Father of The Beano'

While The Beano was the work of many talented writers and illustrators, if any one person is deserving of the accolade of creator, it is R.D. Low.
Recounting the origins of The Beano is a tale that starts not long after World War One, but don't be alarmed, this is no dry history lesson. This is the tale of an unsung genius who always preferred to avoid publicity and work his magic from behind the scenes.

Robert D. Low was a journalist for the large publishing house, D.C. Thomson & Co. Ltd. He joined them as an 18 year-old trainee in 1913. Eight years later, he was Managing Editor of Children's Publications and launching the first of a series of five boys' story papers — The Adventure, Rover, Wizard, Skipper and Hotspur. They would come to be known as the 'Big Five' and were the top sellers of their time — an amazing achievement considering Robert Low had also been overseas fighting in World War One during this time.

Low then turned his vision and drive to producing another series of papers. This time they would be 'funnies', where the emphasis would be on humour. The Dandy comic was launched in 1937. Months later, The Beano arrived. Both comics were an instant success. A year later and The Magic comic appeared — yes, another 'Big Five' was being built, this time of cartoon comics. Only the horror that was World War Two stopped this push for market supremacy.

For The Beano, Low was very hands-on with the selection of artists and writers. He appointed George Moonie, an energetic young man, as Editor. Together they brought in a style of humour that was powerful and visual. The characters they designed scorned all officialdom and authority in the shape of parents, police officers and teachers. This was Low's mantra and it formed The Beano's strongest appeal to children.

ONE IN A MILLION

Beano No. 272 // 1st December, 1945

The next stop on our journey through Beano history is No. 272 from December, 1945. What is it that makes this particular issue so special? This was the first Beano to sell more than one million copies! The Beano's sales ledgers from the time record the sales in meticulous detail, as you can see here:

	.. 17. 7383	
Restricted output now 1,065,000	Dec 1. 8847	
	.. 15. 8860	
	.. 29. 8861	
	1946	
	Jan 12. 8860	

The note to the far left remarks upon the lifting of print restrictions to 1,065,000 copies/issues, virtually all of which were sold. It was a milestone that would probably have been broken earlier but for one thing — World War Two.

With the outbreak of hostilities in 1939 came paper rationing, which saw The Beano enter into a fortnightly publication schedule, on sale on alternating weeks with The Dandy in 1941, and reduce its page count from 28 to 12 in 1942. The Beano provided a morale booster for displaced children, as this letter from reader Walter Hubert told the Beano team from 6th October, 1941:

" I thought it would give you a little pleasure this letter about the Beano, which I like very much." "I all-ways order Beano of-course, otherwise my comic will be sold-out long-ago." "As soon as I come home from after-noon school I start reading the Beano." "I am a jewish refugee nine years old, and came to this country, three days before the war broke out."

The Beano was also vocal in its support for the war effort, with Hitler portrayed in a variety of deprecating comic styles. Intercepted wartime records of a planned German invasion stated that a number of prominent newspaper editors were to be captured and made answerable for the crime of 'gross disrespect'. The Editor of The Beano was included among the names.

D.C. Thomson's Meadowside offices in Dundee, pictured in 1939.

With The Beano facing an existential threat from across the channel, staff being called up for service and illustrators taking cover from Luftwaffe bombs, it was a wonder that the comic continued to be made at all.

The editorial team found The Beano office in Dundee surrounded by sandbags, and soon were being sent far afield. **Editor, George Moonie,** joined the Royal Marines, and was joined overseas by a number of colleagues.

Ron Fraser, Chief Sub-Editor of The Beano, was the hands-on gaffer who made sure the comic production was running smoothly and on time, encouraged artists and staff to maintain high standards. Ron answered to George Moonie.

Iain Chisholm, The Beano Sub-Editor, was one of the experienced editorial staff. All stories were written by freelance scripters and authors at this time. The Sub-Editor would manipulate the storylines before sending them to be illustrated.

The illustrators, working freelance across the U.K., faced problems of their own. Eric Roberts, illustrator of Good King Coke, shared this tale with the office in a letter dated 9th December, 1940.

> I hope that it is only a coincidence but every time you tell me to draw Messerschmitts something happens. Last night was the worst night we've had for weeks and just as I was drawing in the "CRUMP" in Coke's second picture, "Plonk" sounded just outside the window and there blazing away merrily was the nastiest little Incendiary you've ever seen. We got it out before it could do any damage and I don't think that they dropped anything else but fire bombs last night.

Reg Carter lived in Sussex during the Blitz, and had a similar tale to tell in a letter to the office on 13th September, 1940:

> Scores of the 'planes passed this way nightly, absolutely in a line over my house, one or two bombs dropped, but up to present just outside my Sector. Have been up 2 nights out of three, for over a period, getting to bed about 5.30 a.m. the nights I am on duty, saw more dog fights during the week in daytime, also one German coming down.
> Am sending finished sketch to No. 133 and will get on with other and forward at earliest.

By this point in the war, the air raids had been a 'normal' part of life for those living and working near the nation's capital and Carter's letters from this period treat them as business as usual. Here's the Big Eggo comic strip that Carter talks about, as it appeared in The Beano:

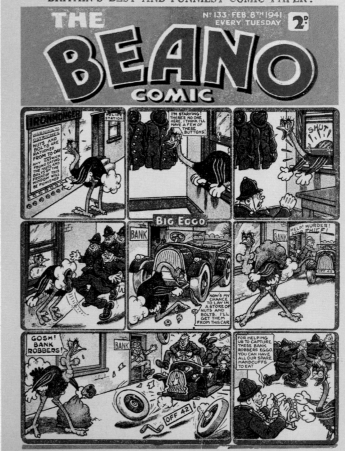

Before going to press, the Sub-Editor had to check and correct all the finished strips and pages.

Ernest Ritchie was another Sub-Editor on the team at the time. As a trainee Sub-Editor, he would be the office junior, running all sorts of errands, whether to do with work or not. This was seen as part of the learning curve of office life.

Fortunately all four returned to the company at the end of the conflict. In their absence, it was left to those either too old or too young to enlist to make the comic, led by Adventure Editor, Stuart Gilchrist.

The readers, too, were asked to asked to play their part in the war effort. Not a week went by without Big Eggo, Pansy Potter or Lord Snooty encouraging the readers to recycle paper. This made the comics themselves a valuable commodity, and children would trade their collections with each other. Copies would be swapped between several friends before eventually succumbing to the weekly reminders contained within.

This recycling meant that Beano copies from the early '40s are now extremely rare collectibles, exchanging hands for hundreds of pounds.

— Don't make paper aeroplanes with your old comics—

NO! TOM THUMB ISN'T CRAZY!

He knows that if you don't save waste paper you'll be helping Hitler!

DON'T WAIT TILL IT COMES TO YOU — *Go To 9t!*

This recycling message even became part of the comic strips themselves, such as Lord Snooty to the right and Big Eggo below.

The Beano didn't mark V.E. Day itself, most likely due to early print deadlines, but the sales ledgers of the time note the gradual lifting of paper rationing and the impact this had on sales. The sales would continue to climb to a peak of nearly 2 million with the 22nd April, 1950, edition as The Beano was about to enter one of its most creative and successful periods.

George Moon

Editor 1938 - 1959

The man selected to be The Beano's first Editor was a kid — a 'whizz kid'. George Moonie had started work with D.C. Thomson as a 16 year old, straight from school. Within five years he had risen to be Chief Sub-Editor of The Wizard and three years later was made Editor of his own comic — The Beano. At 24 years old he was the youngest Editor, a record which still holds true today. His five-man staff were even younger.

In an interview, George Moonie described his new Beano: 'It wasn't the first comic on the market. There were quite a few others but it was a particular style of comic. A percentage of the pages was given over to pure fun — these were the cartoons. There were prose stories for reading and a new picture adventure story. It was a mix of fun and drama, quite a comprehensive production, really, and a lot of work to produce — we worked all sorts of hours. Our aim was to beat other publications by being a better product. We had a lot of competition, in-house competition, even. The Dandy comic was first on the market and had a higher established sale than The Beano but the battle cry was, 'Let's beat The Dandy' — it took us a long time to beat The Dandy.'

George Moonie had been in the Editor's chair for just over a year when World War Two broke out. In 1941, Moonie joined the Royal Marines, leaving The Beano in the hands of a skeleton staff.

Moonie quickly rose to the rank of Captain and was in charge of an assault craft in the Normandy landings of 1944. He would end the war with the rank of Major. Obviously, George Moonie was quite an exceptional soldier. However, in an interview with film director David Puttnam years later, Moonie remarked that he thought The Beano's Lord Snooty did much more to save Britain than he ever did.

The war ended and Moonie returned to editing The Beano in 1946. He oversaw three difficult years where wartime shortages continued to keep The Beano fortnightly and a very small ten pages in size.

To great celebrations, the restrictions were lifted in 1949 and Moonie masterminded a new golden era for The Beano. A year later, The Beano was selling very close to two million copies per week. Famous cartoon strips were launched under Moonie's leadership — Biffo the Bear, Dennis the Menace, Minnie the Minx, Roger the Dodger and The Bash Street Kids, to name a few. George Moonie continued to edit The Beano until 1959 when he was given the role of developing a stable of girls' comics for D.C. Thomson. He launched Judy in 1960 and Diana in 1963. Later in the '60s, Moonie joined the senior management team and he replaced the legendary R.D. Low as overall Managing Editor in 1974.

B

Beano No. 452 // 17th March, 1951

What was the big news in The Beano No. 452, dated 17th March, 1951? You could be forgiven for thinking that it was 'Jack Flash is coming'. The flying boy from the planet Mercury was returning the following week, probably via the planet Krypton.

The really big news was inside on page five, where readers met the world's wildest boy for the first time… Dennis the Menace!

Dennis the Menace started life as an idea from Beano Editor George Moonie. He took his name from an old music hall song whose chorus went, 'I'm Dennis the Menace from Venice.'

It was the job of Chief Sub-Editor Ian Chisholm and illustrator David Law to turn this name into The Beano's newest star. Moonie chose Law due to his work on 'The Wee Fella', a comic strip that had appeared in The People's Journal, and whose main character was a cheeky youngster.

The Wee Fella

Struggling to find the right tone in the busy office, Chisholm and Law decided instead to have a brainstorming session at St. Michael's Inn, a hotel, bar and restaurant a few miles from The Beano office. The outcome of the session was a pencil drawing on the back of a cigarette packet. A legend was born!

DAVID LAW

In the early 1950s, artist David Law was already working as a cartoonist for D.C. Thomson, with most of his cartoons and illustrations appearing in newspapers and magazines. Impressed by his 'Wee Fella' strip, the team worked with Law to create a character for The Beano — he was called Dennis the Menace and would become the best-known boy in Britain. Law drew this naughty scamp in his all-action style and used minimal backgrounds to increase the idea of speed.

Law's distinctive Dennis strips were ground-breaking in style as nothing like this had been seen in comics before. They inspired a new wave of young cartoonists to send their work in to The Beano.

The First Dennis The Menace!

This is the original artwork drawn by David Law in 1951, complete with the comments marked by the editorial staff. Law drew the artwork at double the size it appeared in the comic, allowing for much greater detail in his expressions.

Law drew hundreds of strips but was rarely happy with his completed work. The finished drawn pages would be received by the Beano team covered in patches where he had redrawn characters, often their expressions. It was all beautiful work but he was a

perfectionist. These patches are still visible on the original artwork above. This small, half-page strip was a low-key start for Dennis, who would go on to become The Beano's most popular and recognisable character over the following decades, starring in fiction books and four animated television series!

Red and black?

His distinctive red and black jumper did not make its first appearance in the comic until the 5th May, 1951.

With the stripes now in place, Dennis's growing popularity can be measured by his prominence in the comic. First, he joined The Beano's masthead on the 18th January, 1958, before he took over the cover in 1974, replacing the 'World's Wildest Bear' (Biffo) with the 'World's Wildest Boy', where he has remained ever since.

David Sutherland

David Sutherland started his art career working in the studio of a Glasgow advertising agency. He would draw whatever the advert required — some days it would be gooseberries and plums for fruit jar labels, other times it would be massive portraits of the film stars of the day. Sutherland did a lot of these huge adverts that were placed in the foyer of cinemas. In an advertising agency, the artists had to be versatile and the young Sutherland was one of the best. He came to draw for The Beano via an art competition that D.C. Thomson was running. Sutherland's entry didn't win but it got a terrific reaction from the comics department, who promptly persuaded him his future was with The Beano.

In 1962, Sutherland was asked to draw The Bash Street Kids. Was he successful? Well, he's still drawing them 56 years later.

In 1969, the sudden death of legendary comic artist Dudley D. Watkins stunned The Beano. Watkins was their cover artist, drawing Biffo the Bear every week. Once again Editor, Harry Cramond called on Sutherland. Watkins' style was different again but Sutherland produced beautiful Biffos that could have been by the maestro himself. When David Law, Dennis's original artist, was forced to hang up his pencil due to ill health, Cramond turned once again to Sutherland. Sutherland took over the weekly Dennis and Gnasher pages and made them his own. It was 1972 and Sutherland was drawing the cover story and the two top strips for The Beano. What was more extraordinary was that they all were drawn in completely different styles.

No single artist has done more than David Sutherland to keep The Beano as the King of Comics. If this unassuming, ever helpful, prodigiously talented man can be summed up in one word it is quite simply — genius!

James Hansen

In the '80s the whole UK comic market was in trouble, with publications losing popularity and sales to digital games and animated series. The London-based publishing house of IPC/Fleetway had quite dramatically cut the number of comics it was producing. Their Head of Comic Production, Bob Paynter, contacted The Beano and Dandy Editors telling them that several of his artists were now available to take on work if any was available. Several quality cartoonists started freelance work with The Beano and The Dandy this way — James Hansen, Terry Bave, Sid Burgon and Trevor Metcalfe. All were good professionals and used to working with weekly deadlines.

Brighton-based James Hansen was a great favourite with Beano Editor, Euan Kerr. He liked Hansen's beautiful clean drawing line and the way he could capture the movement and characteristics of kids in action. Hansen drew a lot of Dennis the Menace strips, all to a high standard. He could turn his hand to illustrating any of The Beano characters, a proper old-fashioned production artist — not that his style was old-fashioned. In fact, quite the reverse.

Hansen always made his kids look as though they belonged to today, his school scenes well-observed and modern looking. Having an artist like Hansen was invaluable as it let the regular weekly artists get a break in the punishing week-on-week schedule. When Kerr left the weekly Beano to launch the monthly BeanoMAX he chose Hansen to draw the Wallace and Gromit series. This work had to be top drawer as it was scrutinised by Aardman Editors to make sure the drawn characters were exactly like the original animated versions.

At this time, Alan Digby took over running the weekly Beano. Hansen was already drawing another strip, called Gordon Bennett. It was a terrific-looking strip. Alan always thought Hansen's open style lent itself to colouring very well and so it proved.

Barrie Appleby

And he drives everyone bananas.

Barrie Appleby drew quite a number of Dennis the Menace weekly strips before and after he took over drawing Roger the Dodger in The Beano. Appleby was selected because he was no newcomer to drawing Dennis. During the '80s he had drawn a series of fun comics called Beano Superstars — 32-page-long stories and most of them featured Dennis the Menace.

However, Appleby was probably best known at D.C. Thomson for drawing the terror toddlers Cuddles and Dimples for The Dandy. They became cult characters and even ousted Desperate Dan from the cover for a spell.

When drawing Dennis, Appleby would use his trademark bold character outline, giving Dennis great impact on the cover. He then would follow up with radical page layouts, especially if there was an all-action scene. It gave the Dennis strip a very modern look.

Appleby is a pleasure to work with, and can be relied upon to deliver everything the office asks for in double-quick time. He does this by starting work at his drawing board at 6am — he once said that with it being so quiet in the early morning he could get his day's work done by noon. He likes to encourage budding artists and many have visited his cluttered studio in Suffolk for words of wisdom.

Nigel Parkinson

Nigel Parkinson is a Beano boy and comic fan, who lives and breathes the art form. Also he happens to be the most prolific Beano cartoonist working today. Parkinson, a Liverpudlian, has been drawing Dennis since 1999, as one of a select band of artists producing the strips. In 2012, The Beano commissioned Nigel to become the sole official Dennis and Gnasher artist. This was good for both Parkinson and Dennis. It ensures the image of Dennis and Gnasher is always accurate — especially important now they are not just a cartoon strip in a comic. Dennis and Gnasher are featured in animation, advertising, marketing and merchandising.

The way images are required nowadays is very different from David Law's pen and ink drawings on paper in 1951. Parkinson has embraced and managed the new technology required for producing Dennis in 2018. However, being a true comic enthusiast, Nigel is well aware of The Beano's history and the huge part he now plays in it. The continuing development of The Beano is very important to him. To this end, Parkinson, often accompanied by his colourist, Nika, travels many, many miles attending comic cons and fairs. They are Beano ambassadors, and the media go-to-guys for all things Beano.

Parkinson appreciates his position as Beano artist for it was not always so. As a young man, he struggled to make his name in cartooning. He worked long hours drawing for many differing publications and survived all sorts of editorial knockbacks, trusting that the big Beano break was just round the corner. To him, The Beano was the King of Comics — the place he was heading for.

Reading this you might think that Parkinson is only drawing Dennis and Gnasher — not so. This artist also illustrates Minnie the Minx, Bananaman and The Bash Street Kids. On occasion he can be asked to draw as many as 20 pages of comic strips in a single week.

As The Beano continues to flourish, Parkinson has had a huge hand in gradually modernising many iconic characters while keeping them instantly recognisable.

Harry Cramond

Editor 1960 - 1984

Harry Cramond was The Beano Editor from 1960 until his retirement in 1984. He joined D.C. Thomson's Adventure title in 1937 and worked there until he was called up for active service during World War Two. Cramond became a Battery Sergeant Major and fought with the 8th Army in the famous battle of El Alamein. On returning to D.C. Thomson after the war he moved on to the now-established comics division, where he became Chief Sub-Editor on The Beezer. He had a rather fierce reputation among The Beano's staff, who affectionately called him 'The Grizzler'.

Steve Bright, who worked under Cramond in the late '70s, describes him: 'To me, as an 18-year-old fresh out of school a few months before, he was a giant of a man, commanding great authority and respect, and occasionally an amount of unwarranted fear from all those around him. You might imagine that the office which produced The Beano would be a veritable fun factory, full of laughter, anarchy and chaos. The Beano was a serious office in which to learn the serious trade of creating kids' comics, and Harry's reign as Editor was the reason why. I loved my time in The Beano, and learned so much in those formative months, much of which still stands me in good stead to this day.'

Editing The Beano during the swinging '60s, Cramond was faced with a dilemma: some of the top Beano cartoonists had decided to leave for pastures new. Cramond had to find a new team to take over drawing The Beano favourites, including David Sutherland and Jim Petrie who would go on to be mainstays. In his quiet and calm way, he did this wonderfully well and the look of the iconic comic remained intact.

The Beano that we recognise today took shape under Cramond's eye. He moved Dennis to the cover of the weekly Beano in 1974, and launched the Dennis the Menace Fan Club in 1976. Dennis's stable of pets increased further in 1979 when Rasher arrived. Over the years, Cramond introduced many different characters to the comic but two of his great favourites were both Billys — Billy Whizz and Billy the Cat.

Cramond was in charge when The Beano Annual reached new heights of popularity. He also oversaw the launch of the incredibly popular Beano Summer Specials and Beano Library mini comics.

Harry Cramond masterminded The Beano's 1,000th and 2,000th special birthday edition comics and it was poignant that this popular Editor passed away on the week The Beano reached its 3,000th issue milestone in January, 2000.

FREE INSIDE

Beano No. 954 // 29th October, 1960

The Beano

ANOTHER FREE GIFT INSIDE!

3ᴰ

No. 954—OCTOBER 29th, 1960

EVERY THURSDAY

BIFFO THE BEAR

SNIFF!

WATCH ME GET A BULL WITH EVERY ARROW, BUSTER.

NINE ARROWS LATER

FISSS!

HO! HO! HO! YOU'VE HIT EVERYTHING *BUT* THE TARGET, BIFFO!

I'LL KEEP YOU IN SWEETS FOR A WEEK IF YOU CAN GET EVEN *ONE* ARROW IN THE BULL!

PLONK!

After the war, The Beano went from strength to strength in the 1950s, hitting a peak sale of nearly 2 million copies!

Although paper rationing had ceased many years before, it wasn't until the early 60's that The Beano's page count began to increase again. In 1948 The Beano's pagination was boosted to 12 pages which then rose to 16 pages by October, 1960. This would be marked by a price increase, so to soften the blow to children's pockets, Editor Harry Cramond decided The Beano would include free gifts for the first time in over 20 years.

Free gifts had arrived with The Beano before, with the very first issue in 1938 including a whoopee mask. The only first edition of The Beano complete with whoopee mask thought still to exist was sold for £6,200 in 1999.

The free gifts had ceased due to the industrial demands of World War Two, while the phenomenal success of the 1950s meant that extra marketing was unnecessary. Their return was a welcome surprise for readers.

Photo credit: Jackie Ellis/Alamy Live News

The meaning of the 'whoopee mask' name is lost to time. It clearly didn't make a sound like a whoopee cushion, and while we can theorise that it took its name from the western strip, 'Whoopee Hank', Hank himself did not wear a mask.

The April Fools' Day issue in 1939 came with a free Big-Bang Fun-Gun. This was made from cardboard and made a 'bang' noise when flicked. It would form the basis of the Gnasher Snapper 45 years later.

The first free gift of the 1960s was the Beano Snorter, a modelling balloon that made a rasping sound as it deflated. While no examples of the Snorter exist, the advert from the preceding week gives us some idea of what it looked like. The Beano staff at the time would spend hours trying to think up names for the freebies, since unusual and distinctive names like 'Flying Snorter' were not always easy to come by.

Advertised the same week was The Beano Clickitty Clicker. This was a small handheld device made of tin that would click when pressed. Parents of the time probably remember it as one of the most annoying things in the world. A sentiment not shared by the readers!

FREE
TO ALL BOYS and GIRLS

The Beano
FLYING SNORTER
THE SUPER JET-PROPELLED SQUAWKING BALLOON
IN THE BEANO
The Famous Comic Paper — 16 Pages! 3D
— OUT NEXT WEEK —

THIS ENVELOPE CONTAINS
The BEANO
CLICKITTY CLICKER
FIX THE TONGUE INTO THE SLOT
SLOT
TONGUE
IT DOES NOT "CLICK"
REFIX IT WITH THE
IDE UPPERMOST

FREE
TO EVERY BOY and GIRL

CLICK! CLICK! CLICK!
CLICK! CLICK!
CLICKITTY CLICK!

DENNIS the M

The BEANO
CLICKITTY CLICKER
THE SUPER, SOUND-EFFECTS TOY
IN THE BEANO
The Famous Comic Paper — 16 Pages! 3D
— OUT NEXT WEEK —
— OUT ON THURSDAY —

DENNIS THE MENACE

It would be impossible to list every free gift from The Beano's history, but here are some of the highlights from over the decades.

From April, 1980, the Gnasher "Beano" Glove Puppet was made from plastic. It was great news for Beano fans, who could now keep their favourite menace hound close to hand, to assist in the gnashing of teachers, posties and parents alike.

GNASHER

"BEANO" GLOVE PUPPET

ANOTHER GREAT FREE GIFT FOR "BEANO" READERS NEXT WEEK (ISSUE DATED APRIL 26th)

GNASHER "BEANO" GLOVE PUPPET

YOU'LL HAVE LOADS OF FUN WITH GNASHER ON HAND!

In September, 1984, the Gnasher Snapper arrived. This remains The Beano's most popular free gift, and was originally made in D.C. Thomson's print works at West Ward, Dundee. It was a piece of card about the size of a hand to which thin brown paper had been gummed down on two edges. Once folded and held, a flick of the wrist created a loud bang! This gift proved so popular that the comic used it several times over the years, including for the 60th anniversary in 1998.

The Snapper is no longer used in the comic today, as the sound of the bang is loud enough to fail the health and safety checks for modern children's toys.

One of the best-remembered free gifts was the double-sided poster given away with The Beano's 50th birthday issue.
The reverse side carried a history of the comic to that point, sharing old covers, characters and comic milestones from across the years. This proved so popular that the same was done in 1991 for Dennis's 40th birthday. Likewise, Dennis's history in the comic was covered in some detail on the reverse, including a new comic adventure based upon 'This Is Your Life' that included a caricature of Michael Aspel and the famous big red book.

FREE GIFTS AND THE BEANO
THE EARLY YEARS

In the early years, The Beano, like most comics of the time, used free gifts either attached to the cover or placed inside to induce the prospective buyer to purchase that comic rather than any of the others. The hope was that the buyer would be so entertained by the comic after the gift was either eaten or played with that they would be inclined to continue buying it every week.

Unlike today's comics that, with the exception of The Beano, have freebies every issue, the early covermounted gifts were seasonal. The hard times for all kids' publication were over mid-winter and especially the Christmas period. Comics were certainly non-essential when family budgets were stretched with keeping the home warm and the expense of Christmas. Over this period sales fell every year.

Publishers of kids' comics, not just D.C. Thomson, put a gift out with the comic for a selected week in autumn. This was to boost sales prior to the winter fallback.

They would do the same in early spring, this was to try and regain any sales lost during the winter period.
In the trade they were known as the autumn and spring 'pushes'.

Euan Kerr

Editor 1984 - 2006

Euan Kerr joined D.C. Thomson Publishing in 1969, where he worked on The Hornet comic for a spell before joining the staff of The Beano the following year. Kerr would go on to spend the next forty years with the iconic title.

He did have short spells away from The Beano during the '70s, helping launch The Buzz comic and The Plug (an off-shoot of The Beano). However, he would always return to his first love. He came up through The Beano ranks, serving first as a Sub-Editor, then Chief Sub-Editor before taking over as Editor from Harry Cramond in 1984. Kerr had inherited a legacy of great comic characters which he managed beautifully, keeping them pertinent to the times they were living in without losing any of the charm and humour. With Kerr in charge, The Beano mayhem was also carefully being updated.

He developed new characters such as Calamity James, the unluckiest boy in the world, in 1986, while adding innovations to the long-running characters that he inherited. Roger the Dodger's Dodge Clinic launched the same year, where the readers were encouraged to write to Roger with their problems, which would then be solved by the crafty dodger in comic strip form. When The Beezer ceased publication in 1993, The Numskulls made the short journey to the pages of The Beano. Some of the older characters were retired under his watch, with Lord Snooty making his final regular appearance in No. 2566 in 1991.
Kerr was very much a hands-on Editor and still wrote many of the storylines. He paid particular attention to The Beano Annuals, each year creating mini masterpieces, and this effort showed in the sales.

Kerr was also becoming the public face of the comic. Around The Beano's 50th birthday in 1988, media interest was high and Kerr appeared on Blue Peter. He also joined the Dennis costume character on The Wogan Show, a prime-time programme on BBC One. He even received a letter from Prime Minister Margaret Thatcher, which said: '…over the years [The Beano] has given enjoyment to countless numbers of children. I very much hope that it will continue to delight boys and girls for another 50 years.'

In 1997, Kerr's Beano was voted Best Comic Ever during National Comics Week. Kerr always made sure his Beano was reader-led, so the kids got the madcap fun they expected from their favourite comic. For The Beano's 60th anniversary, the celebration was marked with a further addition to Dennis's family. Bea was born on 19th September, 1998, to date the most recent member of the Menace family. Kerr stayed with The Beano until taking on a management role in 2006. However, he missed the close involvement with the day-to-day running of The Beano and shortly after gave up his management duties to edit the new comic magazine, BeanoMAX.

Kerr retired from the company in 2009 and stated that, with tongue firmly in cheek, 'After 40 years in comics and with my health and sanity almost intact, the lure of the golf course is too much.'

Ⓑ

JOIN OUR CLUB

Beano No. 1768 // 5th June, 1976

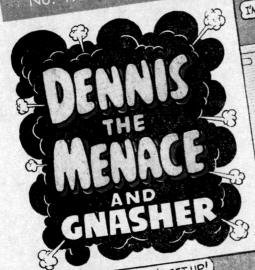

Attention, all Menace fans! I've started my very own fan club — and so has Gnasher! I want you all to join! There's a smashing lapel badge, and a fantastic hairy Gnasher badge, too (see below)! Details of how to join my club at foot of page

On the 5th June, 1976, the Dennis the Menace Fan Club was launched! This was a first for a D.C. Thomson character from any of the comic titles, and was a reflection of just how popular Dennis had become in the 25 years since he first appeared.

In exchange for a 30p postal order, members received a membership card and two badges in a plastic wallet. The card folded out to provide everything a menace might need to communicate in secret with fellow Beano fans, including secret passwords.

The Beano's Chief Sub at the time, Ian Gray, wrote the membership pack, including the codeword greetings — D.I.N.G. (Dennis Is Never Good) and D.O.N.G. (Dennis Owns Naughty Gnasher). Ian Gray was something of a Beano legend, and it was his love of dogs that led to him creating Gnasher, thus establishing an enduring Beano legacy.

Readers were encouraged to write to Dennis, with the promise that 'your problems [would be] answered by a famous problem child.' As an extra incentive, every reader whose letter, joke or story appeared in the comic would win a £1 postal order. This small prize resulted in thousands of letters a week!

As Euan Kerr, Beano Editor from 1984, recalls:

'The Club enrolled over 2,000 new members every week well into the 90s and there were similar numbers of letters and drawings.'

'It was the office junior's job to open all these letters and it took up a great deal of their time. Sometimes we had to call in help from other departments to open the huge volume of mail.'

It wasn't only Dennis's club, of course, as his best friend also received a 'bite' of the action too! The Dennis the Menace Fan Club included 'Gnasher's Fang Club'. Gnasher asked for a 'story about your pet'. This was an extension of the successful 'Pets' Picture Gallery', another idea of Gray's. Morris Heggie, a Sub-Editor at the time, recalls: 'The mailbag of little drawings of pets was several thousand per week — and the popularity lasted and lasted.'

HAIRY BADGE with MOVING EYES

The most popular element of membership was — and still remains — the googly-eyed furry Gnasher badge.

A "DENNIS THE MENACE" JERSEY WILL BE AWARDED TO THE SENDER OF THIS WEEK'S STAR LETTER!

The Dennis the Menace Fan Club pack is fondly remembered by everyone who received it. Included was Dennis's letter to members, which read: 'Dear "Beano" reader, You are now a member of my Fan Club, and here's your membership card to prove it! Fill in the details and keep the card safely in the special wallet. Remember — always wear your club badges. All the best, Dennis. P.S. GRUNT-GNASH-YOWL-SNUFFLE! (That's Gnasher saying, "Welcome to my Fang Club, too!")'

While fans can still remember the secret D.I.N.G. and D.O.N.G. passwords, how many remember the meaning of Gnasher's gnashwords? Secretly supplied by Gnasher, they were for use only by Fang Club Members.

GNOSH! Dinner's ready.

GNASHTY! Dinner's horrible.

GNARK-GNARK! My big sister's always going on at me.

GNOTT GNOTTY I'm well behaved.

GNOTT GNICE I'm not well-behaved.

GNIGHT-GNIGHT Sleep well.

Simon Palmer (millionth member)

METAL BADGE IN BRIGHT COLOURS

THE 2 CLUB BADGES

HAIRY BADGE WITH MOVING EYES

The Dennis the Menace Fan Club would go on to number more than one million members. There was a special prize for the millionth member, as Kerr explained: 'I remember the millionth member being signed up. His name was Simon Palmer from Surrey. He and his family were flown up from London to Dundee and received numerous goodies and also a slap-up feed of mashed potatoes festooned with sausages in typical Beano style.'

The Dennis the Menace Fan Club was finally retired and replaced by The Beano Club in 1998, but the original club remains in the public consciousness nonetheless.

How to wear...

CLUB BADGES

I can stand on my hands.

I've done my homework.

I'm top of my class.

I need my dinner.

I read the "Beano" every week.

I'm foot of my class.

I didn't wash my neck this morning.

I'm a secret "Beano" reader

Famous Fans...

The club went on to count some famous faces among its members. Paul Gascoigne was one, who counted Mars Bars and The Beano as his two favourite things, plus TV presenters Timmy Mallett and Keith Chegwin. John Cleese even wrote to the office to mark The Beano's 50th anniversary in 1988.

Timmy Mallett in The Beano office

Keith Chegwin with Editor Euan Kerr

JOHN CLEESE

9th July 1986

Dear Euan Kerr,

John Cleese thanks you for your letter and has asked me to give you the following comment for your 50th Anniversary Book.

"Dandy and Beano are for me the only two trustworthy journals in the United Kingdom."

Yours sincerely,

Sophie Clarke-Jervoise

Sophie Clarke-Jervoise
Secretary to John Cleese

John Cleese

Madness

Cameos in The Beano were nothing new — during the war not a week went by without Lord Snooty or Pansy Potter getting the better of Adolf Hitler and Hermann Goering. When teen culture took off in the '60s, the famous faces that joined the characters for a one-off appearance changed accordingly.

The list is a who's who of British culture from across the years, from The Spice Girls, Chris Evans, Simon Cowell, David Tennant and Usain Bolt to Mo Farah and Cristiano Ronaldo. For most, it was a genuine honour for them to 'meet' Dennis, Minnie or The Bash Street Kids. Simon Cowell has his comic appearance framed and hung on his office wall!

In the '80s it was the turn of the Nutty Boys of Madness to appear in a Tom, Dick and Sally strip. As a result, this signed photo was received from the band!

A letter from singer Joan Armatrading to The Beano.

> When I was a young girl I was a great fan of Dandy and Beano, and collected a huge pile of comics. Unfortunately, my Mum threw them out without telling me, and in recent years I've had to spend pounds in collectors' shops buying the same comics that cost me a few pennies when I was a kid.

Joan Armatrading

It's so hard to pick out one character as a favourite. Of course I like the menace cos he's "naughty" but I like little plum + I most like Tom Dick + Sally, because of being in a story with them once. Thanks. I love em all.

Here is the Tom, Dick and Sally to which Joan Armatrading referred. Tom, Dick and Sally was a popular Beano strip in the '70s and '80s, drawn by Dave Jenner and Keith Reynolds.

Mark Hamill

The Dennis the Menace Fan Club's most famous member came from a long time ago in a galaxy far, far away...

Mark Hamill, known for playing Luke Skywalker in the Star Wars franchise, sent a photo to the office of himself reading the comic to his newborn son whilst he was filming The Empire Strikes Back at Pinewood Studios in London. Although the polaroid was never used, his accompanying letter was in the 29th September issue in 1979.

He wrote: 'Dear Dennis, I just wanted to let you know I've been a Beanomaniac since 1976 when I did the first STAR WARS. I just never got around to joining the Fan Club. As of June 25th, 1979, I have a little "Gnasher" of my own by the name of NATHAN ELIAS. It seemed like the perfect opportunity to surrender and join. Enclosed find two postal orders of 30p each — one for me, one for my son Nathan. It would be nice to have father-son Dennis the Menace matching T-shirts so we can fly our colours back in California and show comic-lovers back home just what they're missing.'

As a result, Luke Skywalker became a regular part of the club's marketing, regularly appearing with the comic characters, posing the question: 'We're all members of "The Dennis the Menace Fan Club"… are you?'

The relationship between Hamill and The Beano didn't end there, however. When it became known that Luke Skywalker would be returning to the Star Wars films in The Force Awakens in 2015, the team created a reproduction of the Beano comic in the original polaroid and sent it to Hamill.

MARK HAMILL (STAR WARS) and son, NATHAN

 Hamill posted a recreation of the original to his Twitter, this time with Millie the dog.

Alan Digby

Editor 2006 - 2011

Alan Digby became only the fourth Editor of The Beano when he took over from Euan Kerr in 2006. Digby had a lot of Beano experience, starting there in 1970. In his time as Chief Sub-Editor, Digby felt that after Buster's departure from Biffo the Bear there was a distinct lack of children under the age of five portrayed in the comic.

Digby decided to rectify this by creating a brand new character based on his young daughter, Jayne. This would become Ivy the Terrible. At the same time, Beano freelance artist Robert Nixon was looking for more work, and, as one of Digby's favourite artists, the Chief Sub knew that he was the man for the task.

After travelling to meet Nixon at his home in Yorkshire, the artist sent Digby a proposed character design which featured the terrible toddler with a pan on her head as she hid behind sandbags waiting to jump out and cause mayhem. Digby approved it immediately and so the character was born. Ivy was an immediate success and career highlight for Digby, and was even polled as the fourth favourite character within six months of her introduction!

The role of Editor was not new to Alan, having edited The Beezer back in the late '80s and later controlling the production of D.C. Thomson's ever-popular Broons and Oor Wullie strips.

Digby's shift as Editor of The Beano was short-lived by Beano standards, at only five years. However, his accomplishment of steering the comic into the digital age while retaining its hard-won iconic image was nothing short of brilliant. He did this not by making sweeping changes that may have put the future of the comic in jeopardy but by introducing a series of tweaks to the original style.

He introduced a raft of new artists which freshened things up but insisted they bear in mind the classic Beano look. No easy task. He introduced a genuine Beano first as Laura Howell became the first female illustrator to work regularly on the comic. Her first strip was 'Johnny Bean from Happy Bunny Green', a strip Digby described as 'Trumpton with ASBOs', in No. 3404 on 27th October, 2007.

He also oversaw The Beano's 70th anniversary in 2008, when Nick Park — the creator of Wallace & Gromit and a big Beano fan in his youth — guest edited the issue, which saw the iconic claymation duo join Dennis on the front cover.

The work of a Beano Editor in the 21st century was changing dramatically. Online presence had to be given consideration, as did the selection of covermount gifts that the marketplace demanded. The Beano was also taking its first steps to becoming a multi-platform brand during his tenure.

Digby retired from the company in 2011, having had an amazingly successful forty-one years in the land of comics.

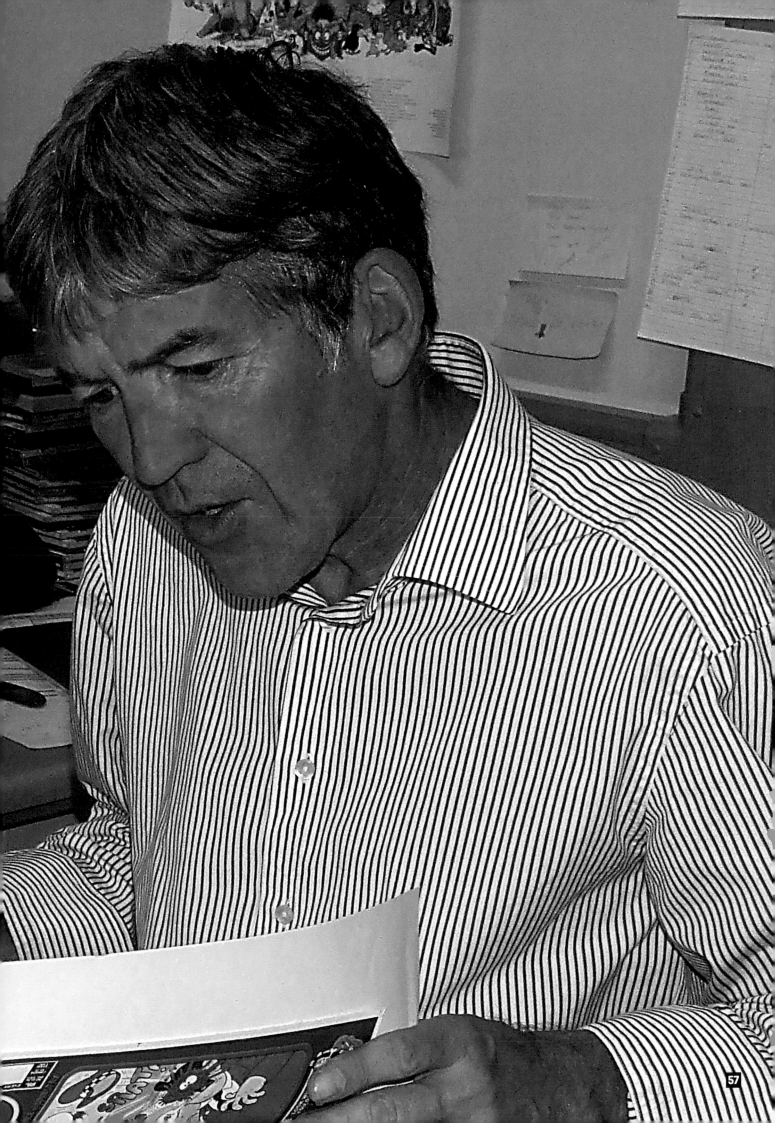

GNASHER GOES MISSING

Beano No. 2280 // 29th March, 1986

THE Beano

HAVE YOU SEEN THIS DOG?

EVERY THURSDAY

16p
I.R. 26p
(inc. VAT)

No. 2280 MARCH 29th, 1986.

DENNIS the MENACE and ~~Gnasher~~

Last week Gnasher went missing. Loyal "Beano" fans are on the march—

WE BEG YOU TO COME BACK, GNASHER

"The Beano" NEEDS GNASHER

We want Gnasher

GNASHER COME HOME

OH, DEAR, WHERE CAN OUR GNASHER BE?

IT'S OK FOR YOU LOT — I HAD TO PUT UP WITH THE LITTLE BRUTE BEFORE HE WENT MISSING!

FOR ONCE I DON'T HAVE TO CHASE THE HAIRY HORROR OFF MY SEAT!

BRR! IT'S NOT NICE AND WARM LIKE IT USED TO BE WHEN GNASHER HAD BEEN ON IT!

HEH! HEH!

HUH!

GNASHER'S NOT HERE TO EAT WHAT YOU DON'T WANT, DAD.

Later— THIS DUMPLING LOOKS HEAVY—I'LL GIVE IT TO GNASHER AND MUM'LL NEVER KNOW.

HE'LL POUNCE ON IT BEFORE IT HITS THE GROUND!

FLIP

ERK! FOUND OUT!

CRASH!

MORE ON BACK PAGE

In 1986 The Beano did the unthinkable and separated Dennis from his best friend Gnasher. The scandalous act occurred in Issue No. 2279 on March 22nd. After a juicy set-up, readers were shocked to discover that Gnasher was in fact missing. This sparked one of the biggest serials the comic had even seen!

Lasting seven weeks, the 'Gnasher Goes Missing' storyline showed a distraught Dennis and co. in their search for the mischievous mutt, while The Beano encouraged fans and readers to write in and join the hunt to find poor Gnasher.

Alan Digby, The Beano's Chief Sub-Editor, was inspired in part by the interest generated by Channel 4 soap opera Brookside. In 1985, the public's imagination had been gripped by the 'Brookside siege' storyline.

This had been an extreme and hard-hitting storyline which saw three people held at gunpoint in a tense, three-episode run that culminated in the death of one of the regular cast members. Looking for a similar hook for the comic, Digby felt that the biggest shock that could befall Dennis was the loss of his best friend.

RADIO 1 DJ MIKE READ WHO WAS ALREADY A DENNIS THE MENACE FAN CLUB MEMBER, TOOK UP THE STORY, APPEALING TO LISTENERS TO LOOK OUT FOR CLUES AS TO GNASHER'S WHEREABOUTS.

WERE YOU A FAN OF THE BEANO GROWING UP?
I was an enormous fan. I loved Lord Snooty, Jimmy & his Magic Patch, Red Rory of the Eagles and General Jumbo and, of course, the naughty boys, Dennis and Roger. I'm still thrilled to have been in Biffo, Dennis, and Billy Whizz comic strips. Magic!

WERE YOU A MEMBER OF THE DENNIS THE MENACE FAN CLUB?
If I say 'DING' and you reply 'DONG', you'll 'gnow' I was!

HOW DID THE TERRIBLE NEWS FIRST REACH YOU THAT DENNIS'S BELOVED DOG GNASHER WAS INDEED MISSING?
It was that moment when the kennel was empty except for a half-gnashed bone! There had to be a good reason why Gnasher would leave a bone!

DID YOU FEEL COMPELLED TO HELP FIND GNASHER?
As a loyal Beano fan and having been in three strips, I felt it my duty to do all I could — like galvanising the Radio One audience!

WHY DO YOU THINK PEOPLE RESPONDED THE WAY THEY DID TO GNASHER'S DISAPPEARANCE?
Everyone loves having fun and so many people read The Beano when they were kids. We collectively have a great sense of humour.

DO YOU HARBOUR A SPECIAL SENTIMENT TOWARDS GNASHER BECAUSE OF THE ROLE YOU PLAYED IN FINDING HIM?
I have a warmth for The Beano in general. But always delighted to help when a pal calls!

The success of the story took Digby and the team by surprise. It was picked up by The Times and even NME, and The Beano editorial staff had to comfort more than one tearful reader who called the office. Theories abounded, including one that he had been kidnapped by The Dandy, since they only had Korky the Cat, who wasn't nearly as funny!

While the search for Gnasher developed each week in the comic, and nationwide due to the efforts of Mike Read and the national press, The Beano team were happy to tease the idea that this could be a genuine parting of the ways. To reinforce the idea, Walter and his dog, Foo-Foo, took advantage of Gnasher's disappearance by replacing him in the comic for the

length of his disappearance with his own comic strip.

Soon the office was inundated with letters from readers who claimed to have spotted clues to Gnasher's whereabouts. Due to the print deadlines of the comic, only a few of these ended up in the comic, such as this one from Steven Crutchley.

Dear Dennis,
Has Gnasher been dognapped? If he has, how much is the ransom? Do you think Gnasher could eat through a wall and escape?
Yours askingly,
Steven Crutchley,
Kendal,
Cumbria.

Dear Steven,
No ransom would be too high for Gnasher's return but I doubt if he's been dognapped — there's no prison strong enough to withstand his Gnashing!
Yours proudly,
Dennis.

Readers' letters...

Dear Dennis,
I think Gnasher is loose somewhere in Newcastle. My dog is a real menace and the other day he was in some bushes and started fighting with something — he normally wins but this time he came running out wimpering, his ear had been Gnashed! I'm sure Gnasher is the only dog who could have done this to him.. Hope you find him soon.....
I've been keeping an eye open for him
Yours searchingly

Dear Dennis
If you don't get Gnasher back next week my mum says you can have our dog Hector. He is half alsatian and half black labrador and he is very nice he has alsatian ears and is black all over if you want him you can have him till Gnasher comes back. He is very good at menacing.
From
Mary Cole age 9

Dear Dennis,
Willy Willy, Ethel Skinner's dog from Eastenders disappeared but he was found in the possesion of someone else. Maybe this has happened to Gnasher,
Yours Hoping You'll Find Gnasherly
Alison Dickson
Worthing
W. Sussex

Dear Dennis,
Please help me, you must bring back Gnasher! I have caught the dreaded Gnashitous, I have started coming out in little Gnashers all over my body and I have grown a tail. The only cure is for Gnasher to come back. Please help aarrgh! oh no! HELP!, GNASH, GNASH, GNASH I've just cantured Gnasha Gnasha Gnasha Gnasha
Yours Gnashingly

(SELINA DEAN)

The story of Gnasher's disappearance gripped the nation in the spring of 1986. Just how did the serial unfold across the weeks? Here's a quick tour:

A week after his disappearance in the 29th March issue, the famous 'Dennis the Menace and Gnasher' dust cloud that introduced the strip sadly had to be changed.

Dennis's Dad initially didn't share the readers' sentiments with regards to the missing pooch as he no longer had to chase Gnasher out of his favourite armchair. However, with Gnasher gone, Dad's problems soon mounted up and he joined the search!

The following week, Digby had a rather brilliant idea to get the readers involved. Already aware of the popularity of the Dennis the Menace Fan Club, and with the knowledge of exactly how many of those famous pin badges were out there, he devoted the cover to 'find Gnasher' badges that could be cut from the cover and stuck to the front of their fan club badges. It was a simple yet brilliant idea!

This was the week that Radio 1 DJ Mike Read got involved, too, and the national press really started to pick up the story.

The sightings started pouring in the following week, the 19th of April, but none of them was Gnasher.

Even Dennis's pig, Rasher, got in on the act. While Rasher was a good pet, he was a rotten Gnasher.

The following week, on the 26th of April, Dennis was starting to get desperate. A trip to the Bureau of Missing People proved fruitless, so Dennis grabbed a spare bone and headed to the zoo — the obvious place to search for a wild animal like Gnasher!

On the 19th April, renowned dog detective Sherlock Bones picked up the trail, but found it only led to a Gnasher fanatic with a collection of furry Gnasher badges. Once again, The Beano team had found a wonderful way to draw the readers' own lives into the fiction of the serial.

But the best was yet to come, at the end of that week's instalment.

We have no idea if kids around Britain howled to the skies that week, but we'd like to think so!

By the time the search reached the 3rd May, all hope seemed lost. Dennis even called on his arch enemy, Walter, for help. But in this final week, a pram arrives at his door. What Dennis found inside was genuinely shocking…

THE BEANO

GNASHER'S BACK!

EVERY THURSDAY

No. 2286 MAY 10th, 1986

16p
I.R. 26p
(inc. VAT)

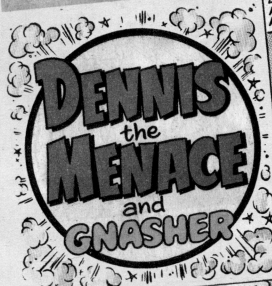

DENNIS the MENACE and GNASHER

Dennis's famous dog, Gnasher, has been missing. Now a pram has appeared at Dennis's door—

WH·WHAT'S IN TH·THERE, DENNIS?

SOFT WALTER

TUG

IT'S A LITTLE GIRL PUPPY!

YIP! YIP!

AAW!

HER NAME'S GNATASHA, AS IT HAPPENS!

YAHOO! IT'S GNASHER!

GNASHER, YOU'RE A DAD NOW!

MEET GNANCY, GNANETTE, GNAOMI AND LITTLE GNORAH!

BLUSH

YIP! YAP!

YAP! YAP!

YIP!

WHAT'S THIS?

YAP! YAP!

YIPPITY YAP!

DAD

GNIP! GNAP!

DAILY

PUPS—MEET YOUR GRANDAD!

GNESH!

HEE·HE SHUCK

LICK

MO BACK

Reuniting Dennis and Gnasher was always the plan but when the storyline began, the ending was still to be decided. Digby considered a number of endings, including Gnasher becoming trapped in an archaeology dig by a huge bone, but Dennis and Gnasher were reunited on the 10th May, with a surprise twist — a litter of pups!

Gnipper, Gnatasha, Gnancy, Gnanette, Gnaomi and little Gnorah were all named by Digby, and even better, ended the serial on an upbeat note, while also generating plenty of publicity for the comic and a wealth of new story ideas.

At the end of the seven-week serial that had seen The Beano generate unprecedented levels of interest nationally, Kerr sent a report to management. He said that while he didn't get the extra readers he'd hoped for, the attention received made the 'soap opera' storyline an ultimate success.

The story didn't quite end there, though. While Gnipper joined his dad in 'Gnasher and Gnipper', still a staple of the comic today, Gnatasha was adopted by Jackie, one of D.C. Thomson's stable of girls' magazines. Aw… we like a happy ending!

LOOK WHO WE'VE FOUND . . .

Remember the gnasty missing Gnasher case in The Beano, where Dennis the Menace's little furry friend disappeared for a whole eight weeks? Well, you'll be relieved to hear he's returned safe and sound . . . but with several pups tagging behind. (Gnaughty dog!)

As you can imagine, they all take after their dad so life in The Beano has become pretty wild! That's why we've stepped in and adopted one of the pups, Gnatashia, as our very own Jackie mascot. We promise she'll have a good home and have more Jackies than she'll have time to read!

Ah, we do like a happy ending.

The Gnasher Goes Missing serial set the gold standard of Beano PR stunts, but it hasn't stopped the team trying to top it over the years.

In 1991, Dennis ditched the red and black stripes for something much more '90s — sunglasses, tracksuit and trainers. He even ditched the catapult in favour of a personal stereo. Of course, this 'new look' didn't survive to the end of the comic.

When The Bash Street Kids celebrated their 40th anniversary in 1994, Kerr came up with the idea of updating the kids. This included closing Bash Street School, sacking Teacher and giving the kids a makeover. It proved to be a successful tactic to get The Beano into the papers, who played along, and much ire was expressed on their letters pages!

More recently, social media has contributed to the comic's publicity as much as the national press. It was in March 2018 that The Beano sent politician Jacob Rees-Mogg a cease and desist letter for infringing upon Beano's copyright — namely that he was 'copying' the style and manner of Dennis's arch enemy, Walter Brown.

Michael Stirling

Editor 2011 - 2012

Michael Stirling started work at D.C. Thomson in 1997, joining the staff of teen magazine Shout. In his role of Celebrity Editor he would interview and arrange photoshoots with popstars and celebrities, such as The Spice Girls and Mariah Carey. His early claim to fame was the time that Carey phoned his home for an after-hours interview from overseas!

His involvement in developing magazine projects saw him move to become the Deputy Head of Children's Entertainment and into professional contact with The Beano for the first time. His work on these projects had given him an impressive insight into the way the audience was changing their media habits and how comics — and The Beano in particular — had to respond to these new challenges.

As The Beano looked to expand into other media platforms, Stirling found himself becoming further involved in the comic until, with the retirement of Alan Digby in 2011, he took up the Editor's chair.

His time as Editor was short but eventful, however, he brought all of his Shout experience to the making of the comic, responding to trends and celebrities with uncommon speed. Highlights included Harry Hill guest-editing 'The bald issue', which saw Dennis lose his trademark spikes for a week, and the gold-foil Ennis the Menace cover to celebrate the achievements of Jessica Ennis-Hill at the London 2012 Olympic Games.

In 2016 Stirling became Head of Beano Studios Scotland. D.C. Thomson launched Beano Studios to deliver mischievous entertainment for kids on multiple platforms including TV, digital and consumer products. Stirling is a spokesperson for Beano Studios, appearing on TV and radio.

B

2,000 AND OUT

Beano No. 3052 // 13th January, 2001

GET NEXT WEEK'S "BEANO" AN' YOU'LL SOON KNOW WHY THEY CALL ME A MINX!

TACKS

This issue saw an ending of sorts, as Minnie the Minx artist Jim Petrie hung up his pencil with the completion of his 2,000th Minnie the Minx strip.

Minnie the Minx had clocked up nearly 50 years in the comic by this point, having first appeared in the corner of page five of The Beano on 12th December, 1953. As you can see to the left, she hasn't changed much, keeping her iconic plaits, beret, and mischievous grin first given to her by Leo Baxendale back in 1953.

Leo Baxendale

Leo Baxendale is frequently named as one of the greatest comic artists this country has ever produced. By Beano standards he did not have a long career drawing for the title but no other artist had such a major influence on its style.

In 1952, Baxendale was a budding cartoonist aged 22 and living in Preston. While reading his younger brother's Beano he became very impressed with the new style of comic art that had come in with the introduction of the Dennis the Menace strip. He sent off samples of his own work to The Beano and after one or two false starts, Baxendale was given a short strip called Little Plum. The scripts were written by The Beano staff and given to Baxendale to illustrate but he added many zany touches to the stories himself. The results were hilarious. The following year Beano Editor, George Moonie, asked Baxendale to do sketches for a female Dennis the Menace character. She was to be called Minnie the Minx. Baxendale did a brilliant job and Minnie evolved from a little six-frame strip to a full page in record time. Minnie was famous for bashing bully boys and Baxendale invented crazy weapons to help her. Just two years into his time at The Beano, Baxendale had two top strips in the comic — but the best was still to come.

By 1954, Baxendale had moved up to Dundee to be close to the D.C. Thomson headquarters. He enjoyed working with the creative young Beano staff in their office. On one such occasion, George Moonie and Baxendale decided to produce a school story, being inspired by looking from the office window across to the High School of Dundee's yard right outside. It was to be a wild, unruly school — Bash Street School! The building, teachers and kids were from Baxendale's imagination and were the perfect crew for his mischievous sense of humour. It was a strip packed with anti-authoritarian unruliness. Just ask their weary teacher, the janitor, and the local police force. The strip was first titled 'When the Bell Rings' and did not become 'The Bash Street Kids' until two years later. The mayhem that started all those years ago still continues today.

Bash Street Kids

In their sixty-year history, The Bash Street Kids have achieved several landmarks of their own.

In 1994, to celebrate the 40th anniversary of the strip, Euan Kerr, Editor at the time, teased readers that The Beano would drastically change the characters and setting in an effort to be more politically correct.

It was, of course, a prank. Inspired by the success of the Gnasher Goes Missing serial in 1986, Kerr wanted to stir the general public up, and even sent a press release to The Times detailing the changes that would be made. This included replacing Bash Street School with Bash Street Academy, firing the school staff and replacing them with robots, making Fatty thin, Spotty being clear skinned, and Smiffy would be intelligent.

While the idea seems too preposterous to have been believed, times were changing at The Beano, as the '90s had already seen beloved characters Lord Snooty and Pansy Potter leave the comic. Kerr explained some were 'too old-fashioned and had little or no relevance to modern readers, which could have easily applied to Teacher's gown and mortar board.

Most of the public did believe it, and a national cry rang out just as it had for when Gnasher went missing. Kerr received 2,500 protest letters, and one girl even collected 407 signatures in a petition to halt the changes. Similarly, Stanwix School in Carlisle ran their own campaign and made posters in an effort to save 'Bash Street Skool'.

Kerr was pleased with the response and publicity generated for the 40th anniversary and, in issue No. 2692, all was resolved when the robot teachers fizzed out and the academy was destroyed, ending the strip with Olive the dinner lady bringing in a celebration cake for the kids.

WAHEY!

In 2013, the 75th anniversary of The Beano saw even more celebration for these troublesome school children, as a lane close to the home of The Beano in Dundee was renamed Bash Street. However, not everyone was pleased with the new street name, as then Editor, Mike Stirling, joked: 'The Beano team are thrilled — well, everyone except Dennis. He's not a happy boy, not at all. He thinks the street should have been named 'Menace Street'.'

Here's Minnie's first comic strip appearance in The Beano dated 19th December, 1953.

MEET MINNIE—*She's horrid, she's awful, she's dreadful*—she's GREAT FUN!

MINNIE THE MINX

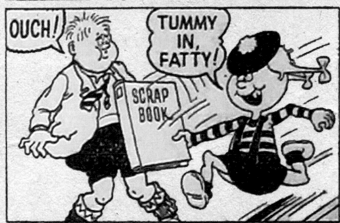

Her stripy jumper made her look even more like a female Dennis the Menace. When her popularity quickly propelled her to a full page in The Beano's iconic red and black colour palette shortly afterwards.

In 1961, locally-based artist, Jim Petrie, illustrated Minnie the Minx for the first time. Petrie would go on to draw Minnie the Minx for the next 40 years, a remarkable feat of longevity that the Editor at the time, Euan Kerr, chose to mark by writing Petrie into the final strip, with Jim's last comic strip panel literally a self-portrait.

Reproduced here is Petrie's original artwork for the strip. The title, sound effects, colour and balloons were added to the artwork by a dedicated team of Colourists and Balloonists who were part of D.C. Thomson's art department.

The editorial staff would use tracing paper to mark the positioning of the balloons and send it with the script to the Photon Department who would transcribe the type in the correct font and size so these balloons could be attached by hand to the artwork by the Balloonists.

This was then combined with the colour, which was also added in house. The finished pages looked like this...

On 11th December, 2013, Minnie celebrated 60 years of Beano fun by ousting the boys and becoming the first female cover star. Although Minnie appeared in six decades of comic strips by this point, she remained as much a minx as ever, with then Editor Michael Stirling remarking, 'We can't quite believe it's Minnie's 60th anniversary. She looks so young!'

Drawn by Nigel Parkinson, the cover features Minnie bursting through Christmas wrapping paper, her hands full of nefarious prank gear, a huge grin on her face, and a balloon reading, 'It's my birthday and I'll MINX if I want to!' As well as the cover, the issue also included a full page showing a delighted Minnie licking her lips feverishly, her hands poised to dig into an aptly red birthday cake!

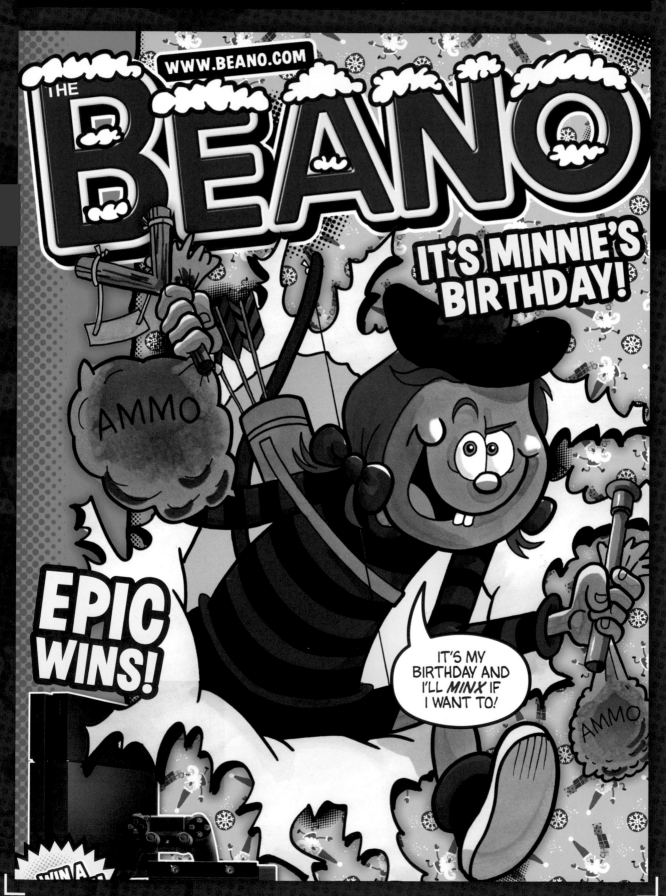

Minnie was immortalised in 2001, when a statue of her was erected in the centre of Dundee. Forever up to mischief, the sculpture catches her primed and ready to fire her slingshot at poor Desperate Dan in front of her.

It's Minnie's birthday this week, so we're all going to sing her a song! You can join in too!

HAPPY BIRTHDAY MINNIE!

Happy birthday to you! You live in a zoo! You look like a monkey, And you smell like one too!

60 YEARS OF MINXING

Now we'd better run before she realises what we said about her!

The third-longest-running character after Dennis the Menace and Roger the Dodger, Minnie's popularity has grown and grown. She's become a regular cover star for The Beano, making her the fourth character to feature solo on the front page after Big Eggo, Biffo and Dennis. Since Minnie's cover debut, many other characters like Roger and Bananaman have followed suit and graced the front of The Beano. Minnie's next starring cover was on the 4th February, 2017, which was shortlisted for Cover of the Year at Scotland's Professional Publishers Association awards.

Minnie's popularity has also paved the way for new female characters to enter the mix. Introduced for the CBBC TV show, Dennis & Gnasher Unleashed, super-athletic JJ and brainiac Rubi have since become regular faces in the comic.

Another popular female character revived in the comic is 1993's The Yeti with Betty, now renamed Betty & the Yeti, which centres on 'The ordinary girl with the extraordinary best friend.' Since 2015, all issues feature her half-page comic strip.

M The Beano's audience is evenly split between boys and girls, and a new generation of female stars is following in the footsteps of Minnie the Minx.

Jim Petrie

During the early '60s, Minnie the Minx's original artist, Leo Baxendale, had stopped drawing for The Beano and was working on new projects.

At the same time a local young art teacher at Kirkton High School, Dundee named Jim Petrie was looking for some freelance work on the side. So, Petrie got in touch with D.C. Thomson's Sparky Editor, Ian Chisholm, who asked to see some of his pencil sketches. Unfortunately, Petrie's art didn't seem to suit to begin with, as Chisholm told him, 'You're trying to be too original, just use the characters we're using. Develop them.' And so he did! Taking over from Leo Baxendale, Petrie quickly impressed Chisholm and R.D. Low, imitating his predecessor's style before adding in his own flourishes, eventually gaining enough confidence from then Beano Editor Harry Cramond to bring in inks instead of pencils! By 1969, Petrie was working solely on The Beano, where he became the regular Minnie the Minx artist and would continue to draw Minnie's weekly adventures for the next 40 years.

Petrie liked to strike up a good partnership with whoever on The Beano staff was writing his Minnie strips. He enjoyed working with Al Bernard in the '60s and '70s then latterly struck up a long-lasting partnership with Beano writer, Craig Ferguson. Both these writers understood that Petrie liked minimal art direction as this gave him more freedom to do the all-action scenes he loved. This was encouraged by Cramond, who didn't like empty space in his comics and was always telling his artists to 'put something here, put something there', making sure every inch was filled with the title's signature zany humour. Petrie didn't have a problem with this — in fact, if Chief Sub-Editor Ian Gray ever said that a script was a bit thin, Bernard would reply 'Jim will sort it.' As a result, Petrie's pages always flowed perfectly because of the independence he was allowed in illustrating them, making him a huge part of every script he was involved in.

He drew very few cartoon strips other than Minnie as Petrie required time to work on his own art, which he exhibited nationally on many occasions. Although he drew the bulk of his Minnies in black and white, Petrie loved colour. He always dressed colourfully and his own paintings showed his mastery of colour. In fact, one of his personal favourites from his work on The Beano was a coloured double page spread of Minnie featuring lots of bright red and orange tomatoes (we can only imagine what the little minx was doing with them!)

Always a class act, Jim Petrie retired in 2001 after completing exactly 2,000 weekly episodes of Minnie. Although no longer working for The Beano, he kept in touch with staff members and was always interested in how Minnie was doing.

Sadly, Jim Petrie passed away in 2014, but his mark on The Beano is still felt today.

Craig Graham

Editor 2012 - 2016

Craig Graham began his career in D.C. Thomson in the same year as his predecessor Michael Stirling, in 1997. However, his route to becoming Beano Editor could not be more different.

The first title that Graham worked on was D.C. Thomson's licensed magazine, Sesame Street, for pre-schoolers. After a year there, he began his first stint working on The Beano, just in time for the preparations for the comic's 60th anniversary. Euan Kerr's big idea for the 60th was the arrival of Bea, Dennis's little sister. However, at this early stage she did not have a name and Graham's first job was to sift through the mountains of mail that the readers had sent in with suggestions to name her.

He moved across the corridor to The Dandy at the turn of the millennium, and was instrumental in the comic's relaunch in 2004. He became Editor in 2006 and oversaw The Dandy's transformation into The Dandy Xtreme, a comic/magazine hybrid, before The Dandy returned to its weekly comic strip roots in 2010.

He became Editor of The Beano in 2012. The new generation of comic talent Graham had discovered in The Dandy's final years joined him on The Beano, unleashing a new generation of wacky writers and illustrators on the readers.

He launched the Beanotown project, which was a massive undertaking to draw all of The Beano's cast into a single location — Beanotown. Like The Simpsons' town of Springfield, this was a large fictional backdrop in which the new writers and illustrators could let their imaginations fly. The other successful launch from his tenure was 'Make Me a Menace'. Having learned from research that the readers longed to be able to join the comic strip fun, 'Make Me a Menace' offered them a simple premise to do so. Readers were asked to submit their 'Menace name' and photo, and each week one would be chosen and turned into a Beano character. This was so popular that it received many thousands of entries in just a few months. If every entry were to be used, it would fill the comic's back page for some 50 years or more.

Graham joined Michael Stirling at Beano Studios after its launch in 2016, where he now oversees the expansion of the comic and its characters across multi-media platforms. He was most recently credited as 'script consultant' on Dennis and Gnasher Unleashed on CBBC and ensured the smooth transition of new characters Rubi and JJ between TV show and comic.

I CAN'T BELIEVE I'V NEVER BEEN HERE BEFORE!
BEWAR
COOL
TRAP
INSI

RECORD BREAKER

Beano No. 3800 // 5th September, 2015

Mention an anniversary or milestone and there are few who would select No. 3,800 as particularly remarkable. However, The Beano's 3,800th issue was notable, as it was recognised as the longest-running comic published weekly by Guinness World Records!

The previous record holder was The Dandy, which ceased publication with No. 3610 in December, 2012. In turn, it had taken the record from Comic Cuts, a publication that had run for 3,006 issues from 17th May, 1890 to 12th September, 1953... which is why you may never have heard of it.

Why did it take such a long time for anyone to notice that The Beano had passed this milestone some way back in November, 2011? The explanation for that is simple. With The Dandy still in continuous publication at that time and some seven months older, no-one stopped to consider that The Beano might ever overtake it.

Despite sharing some of the same staff, as well as countless writers and artists, we're not sure if The Beano's big brother, The Dandy, would have been too pleased to hear about being usurped. But, as with all big brothers, we're certain that The Dandy would put aside any notions of rivalry and be proud of the younger comic.

After all, there is no question that The Dandy's original record paved the way for The Beano's longevity as the torch was passed from one comic giant to another.

This is the cover of The Beano No. 3611 from 12th November, 2011. It was in fact the record-breaking issue, although no-one realised at the time. In 2011, The Dandy was still in continuous weekly publication and showed no signs of ending.

The certificate was eventually delivered to The Beano office at its temporary home at D.C. Thomson's Kingsway building in Dundee, where it was unveiled by Beano legend David Sutherland.

GUINNESS WORLD RECORDS™

CERTIFICATE

The longest-running comic published weekly is The Beano, published by DC Thomson (UK) with 3,800 issues as of 5 September 2015.

World's Biggest Comic

The longest-running comic isn't the only accolade Beano has racked up in its history. On the 16th June, 1988, the comic teamed up with 'Hann-Made' Productions to create the world's biggest comic!

After being approached by the Production's head, David Hann, for a project involving The Beano and Scarborough Beach, Editor Euan Kerr and Beano scriptwriter Al Bernard hopped on a train and headed south.

Hann's original idea was to do something 'big' involving local high schools, incorporating recognisable children's characters into the project. After D.C. Thomson was contacted for permission to use members of The Beano gang, Kerr was delighted to get involved. The project quickly evolved into creating a replica Beano cover (released the same week as No. 2396) drawn on Scarborough South Bay Beach itself, which would attempt to break the Guinness World Record for the world's biggest comic.

GUINNESS BOOK OF RECORDS

THIS IS TO CERTIFY THAT

LARGEST COMIC STRIP

39950 ft² (170 ft x 235 ft)

SCARBOROUGH SOUTH BAY

Organised by CRESCENT ARTS WORKSHOP/BEANO

DONALD McFARLAN   NORRIS McWHIRTER

Donald McFarlan   *Norris McWhirter*

THIS CERTIFICATE DOES NOT NECESSARILY DENOTE AN ENTRY INTO THE GUINNESS BOOK OF RECORDS

THE COMIC WITH
IVY THE TERRIBLE
BEANO
No. 2396 JUNE 18th, 1988
EVERY THURSDAY
20p

Paper guides for the cover were provided for the children by Hann's wife, each square representing five square feet of the beach!

One hundred children and their teachers from ten local schools were recruited to help colour the 39,950-square-feet cover on the beach. Armed with Beano t-shirts and £3,000 worth of vegetable dyes, the youngsters soon set to work to finish the piece within the two-hour window the tide allowed!

To give an idea of scale, each letter in the title was sixty feet high and a single hair on Billy Whizz's head was six feet long! Not only was the record attempt a success, it was even featured in BBC's 'Cheggers Checks It Out'.

Though it washed away, this gigantic feat still left its mark on those involved, and Kerr and Hann remain friends to this day.

The Beano has always enjoyed milestone celebrations…

75th anniversary

The Beano celebrated its 75th anniversary with an exhibition as part of the Southbank Centre in London, where the fictional home of the comic's stars was brought to life.

The exhibition itself brought together previously unseen artwork, The Beano Bar, where you could munch on comic-themed food and drink (anyone for a Splat-a-Pult?), and The Beano Studio where you could have a go at creating your own comic masterpieces (if you dared).

Pictured are Michael Stirling and Dennis cutting the birthday cake, a special commission by Choccywoccydoodah!

At the time of going to press, the comic has notched up 3,940 issues, which means it will strike 4,000 in the summer of 2019. But what is truly remarkable about the comic is that this week and every week onwards, each new issue of The Beano is a record-breaker. While this is a special achievement for us, it is also a special achievement for you, the readers, who have made this possible. So... please treat yourselves to a slap-up feed as we celebrate The Beano's 80th birthday and look forward to the next anniversary and beyond!

The Beano has sold in excess of two billion copies to date — and counting! That's enough comics to stretch all the way to the moon and back.

Covers of the 1,000th, 2,000th and 3,000th issues.

FREE COMPETITION INSIDE

OVER 2000 PRIZES!

EVERY THURSDAY

8p

AND I'LL SHOW YOU A PICTURE OF THE COVER OF THE VERY FIRST "BEANO" ON THE BACK PAGE, READERS!

No.3000 JANUARY 15, 2000. Every Thursday. 52p

THE BEANO

9 770262 246102

John Anderson

Editor 2016 - present

John Anderson is the first non-Scottish Editor of The Beano. Originally from Jarrow, in the north-east of England, he came to Dundee to study animation at the University of Dundee with big dreams of being the next Chuck Jones… dreams that were dashed when he discovered he was much better at writing cartoons than drawing them.

Anderson started work on The Beano in 2004 as the Editorial Assistant, opening the sacks full of mail (back when people used to send physical items through the post!), and working on some of the lesser-known Beano characters such as Les Pretend, Freddie Fear and Gordon Bennett.

After a brief spell on The Dandy in 2006, he joined Euan Kerr on BeanoMAX in 2007 from issue No. 3. He eventually returned to The Beano staff full time in 2010, this time as a fully fledged Magazine Journalist.

During this period, Anderson wrote for virtually every Beano character you could name and even managed to create a few, his favourite being Dangerous Dan.

Anderson was responsible for working with writers and illustrators to create new mini-strip ideas. The short stories proved to be a successful testing ground for new ideas and characters.

In 2016, Anderson made the step up to Editor. Today Anderson leads the comic team as part of a wider multi-platform kids' entertainment brand, as characters move seamlessly from the pages of the comic to digital platforms, TV series and beyond!

While Editors of the past could scarcely imagine what the comic has now become a part of, Anderson's responsibility to bring his team of talented writers and illustrators together to deliver funny, mischievous comic strips that entertain and delight is the very same brief handed to original Beano Editor George Moonie 80 years ago.

As the seventh incumbent of Beano's Editor's chair, Anderson jokingly refers to himself as the 'Sylvester McCoy' of Editors.

B

Now in its 80th year, The Beano shows no signs of slowing down. In 2017, D.C. Thomson sold 1.86 million copies of The Beano which is no mean feat for a print product today. A copy of The Beano is sold every 17 seconds in the UK! Maria Welch, Head of Publishing at D.C. Thomson, comments, 'The children's magazine sector is characterised by frequent launches and closures and it is testament to the enduring appeal of The Beano that today's readers are still being entertained every week by the nation's favourite comic.'

WE LOOK PRETTY GOOD FOR OUR AGE!

Standing out in the kids' section of the newsstand certainly is a challenge, and anyone who has looked at a magazine shelf recently will be familiar with the anarchy and disorder. But anarchy is The Beano's middle name! Every other publication contains similar colour palettes and huge, polybagged packages that are chock-a-block full of projectiles, slime and stickers. Not The Beano. The Beano stands out with 36 pages and only occasionally carries gifts — and it works brilliantly.

The key to The Beano is the cover. Each cover must tick off all the visual cues that kids need to pick up a magazine. We've got eggy pongs! We've got pranks! We've got hilarious cover illustrations! We've got characters you know and love! All the things 6 to 11-year-old kids love are on the cover, just as they always have been.

The editorial team deploy a level of reader understanding and engagement unseen in most children's magazines — a key to the continuing success of the

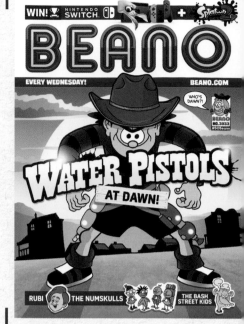

comic. Every issue a reader becomes #SOBeano — they choose jokes, pranks and star letters, read and approve the comic strips and, best of all, become comic strip characters themselves to meet their heroes. It is this keen awareness of children's lives that has ensured The Beano's success yesterday, today and tomorrow.'

Today's Readers

The Beano team work hard to ensure that characters are genuine, authentic and representative of kids today. Today, after decades of being primarily a boys' comic, The Beano's audience is evenly split between boys and girls. This is due in part to the team writing in and creating more female characters, including JJ, Rubi, Betty & the Yeti, Angel Face, Hayley Comet, Holly Wood, Jungle Judy and Zoo-ella. They don't just appear on the internal pages, either — they are front-cover-worthy.

The Beano team...

Back row, left to right: Gary Aitchison (Graphic Designer), Leon Strachan (Design Editor), John Anderson (Editor), Georgia Battle (Editorial Assistant) and Mark McIlmail (Graphic Designer). Front row, left to right: Alexandria Turner (Editor-in-Chief), Claire Bartlett (Content Editor), Michelle O'Donnell (Production Editor), Elaine Skinner (Graphic Designer) and Jen Scouler (Magazine Journalist).

The work doesn't stop at the weekly comic. The Beano Annual has been the best-selling annual in the UK for an entire decade and continues to see off competition from international children's mega-brands. Every year it proudly hits the Top 100 Best Sellers list and the team are already lining up its next best seller.

The Beano's two seasonal issues still remain enormously successful — The Beano Christmas Special and The Beano Summer Special. These are a fantastic opportunity for the team to get really creative, produce a longer story than in the weekly comic, and to reward The Beano's most dedicated fans.

Beano HQ!

In May, 2017, five years after The Beano team were decanted to the D.C. Thomson's Kingsway site, they returned to a refurbished Meadowside building where The Beano was born.

Dundee is currently undergoing a regeneration and the V&A Museum of Design is due to open in late 2018. The Beano is proud to play its part in the resurgence of its home city and to continue to inspire generations of children.